SHOW YOUR TRUE COLORS

SUSAN BUSCHMANN

Coloring is a great form of relaxation. It is a calming activity some people use as a tool for comfort and stress management.

This is my first published coloring book. I have always doodled to relieve tension and hope you find my designs satisfying to color. These abstract designs are all hand drawn compositions in ink.

To purchase more copies, go to Amazon and enter the title… *Show Your True Colors.* Also a very special thank you to my sister Adrienne Begley for helping with the cover by showing her true colors.

Thank you for purchasing this book - check me out on Instagram @Spectator.Art and look for my next book that will be completely mandala designs.

Enjoy!

Susan Buschmann

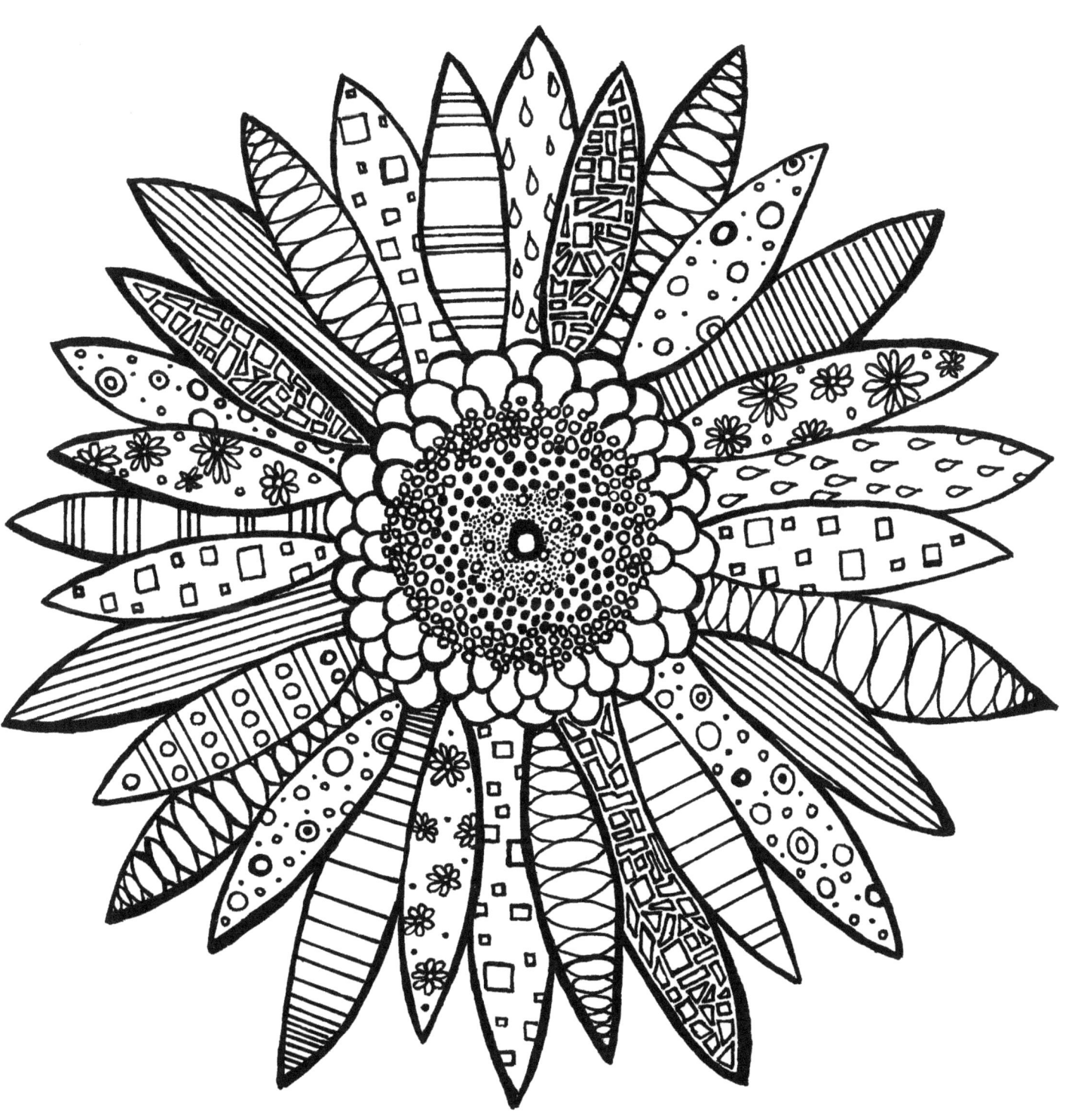

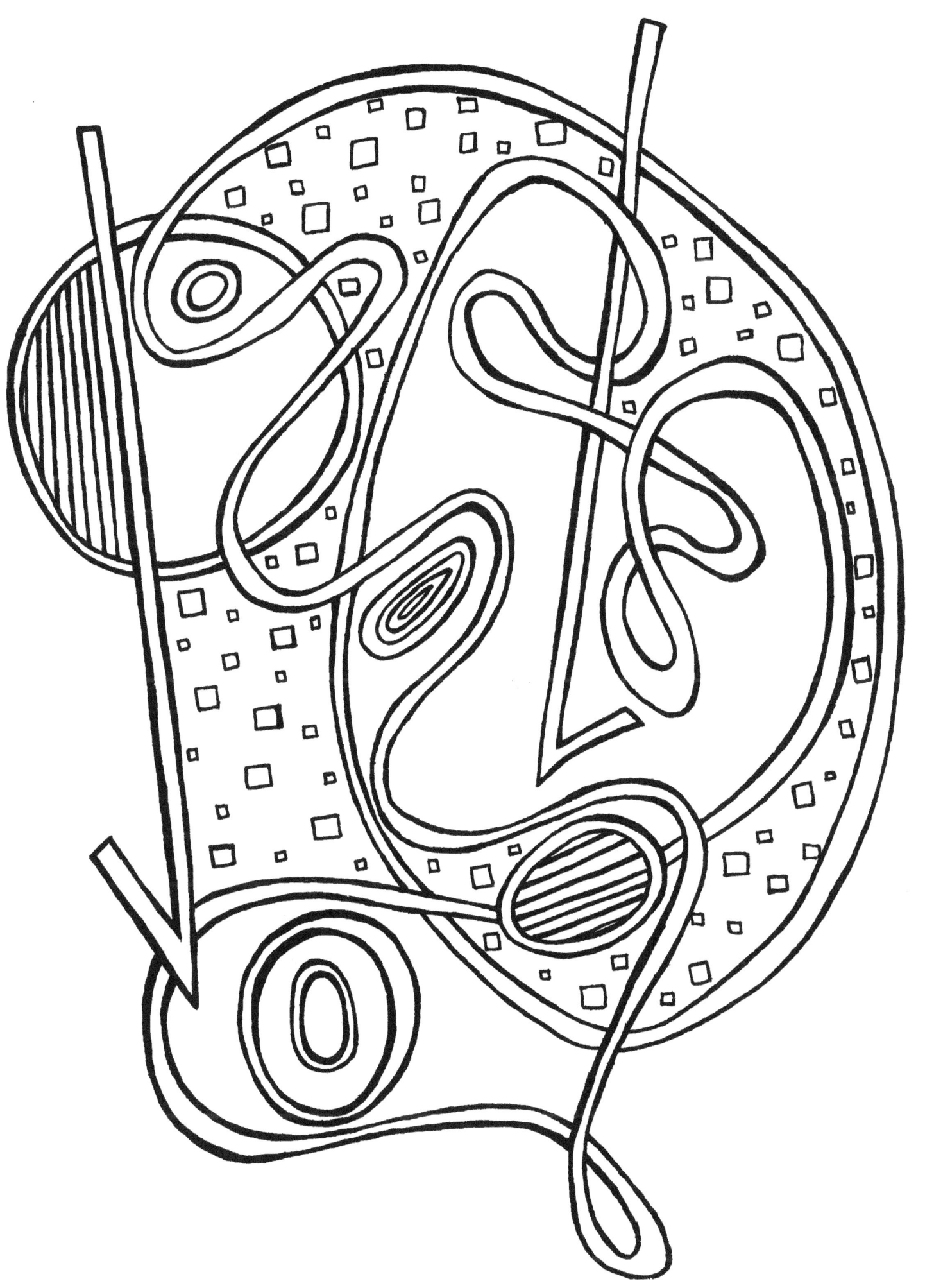

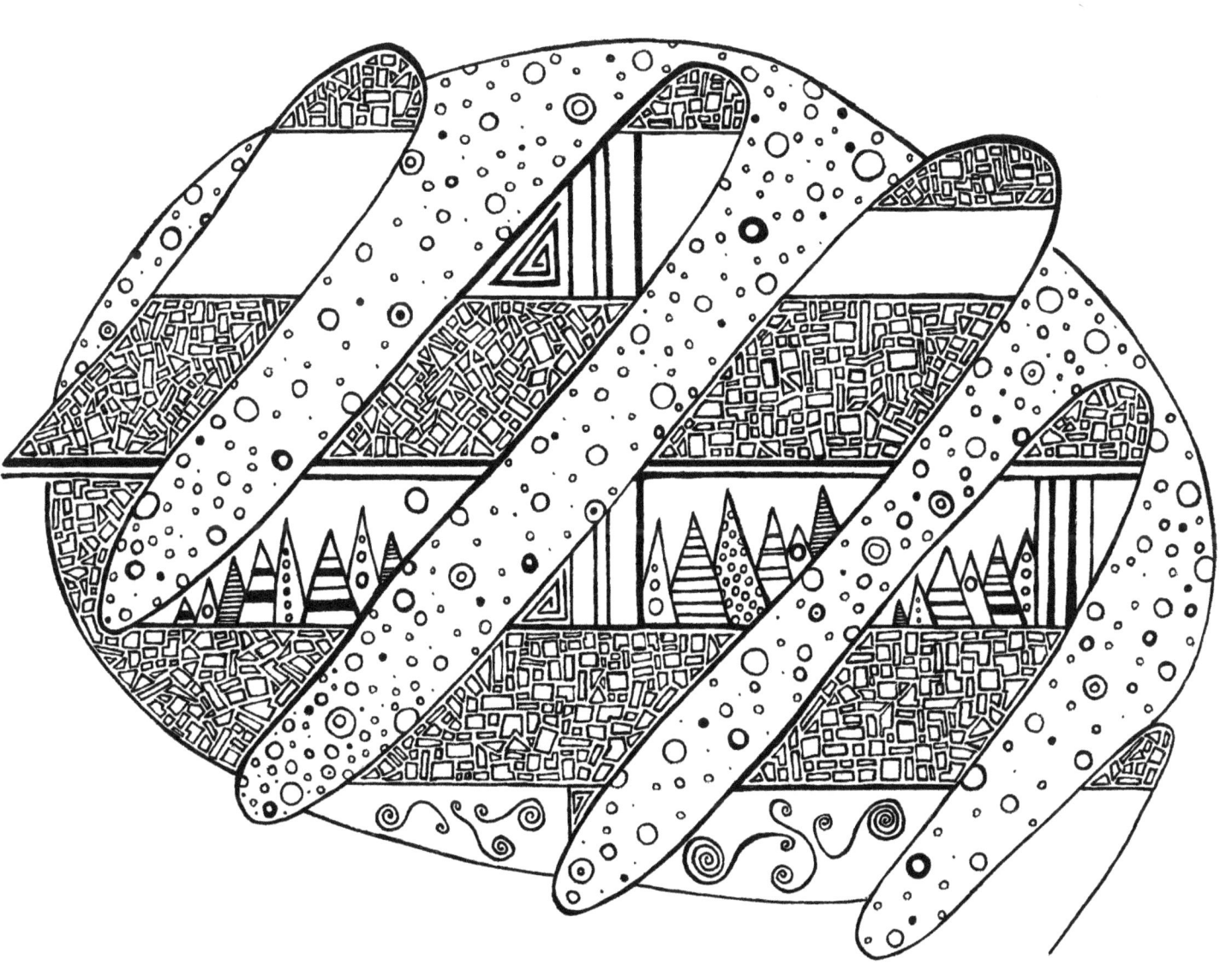

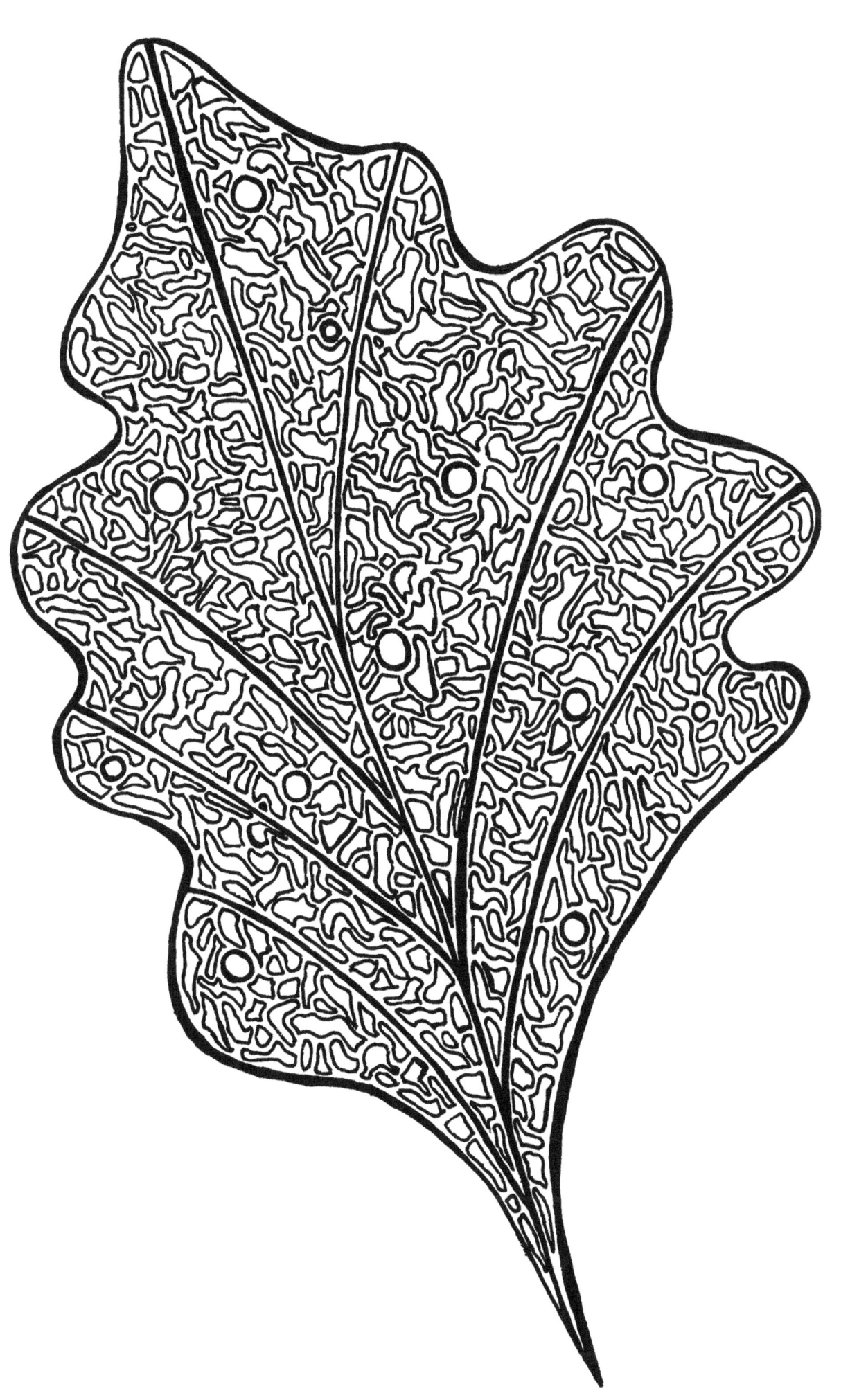

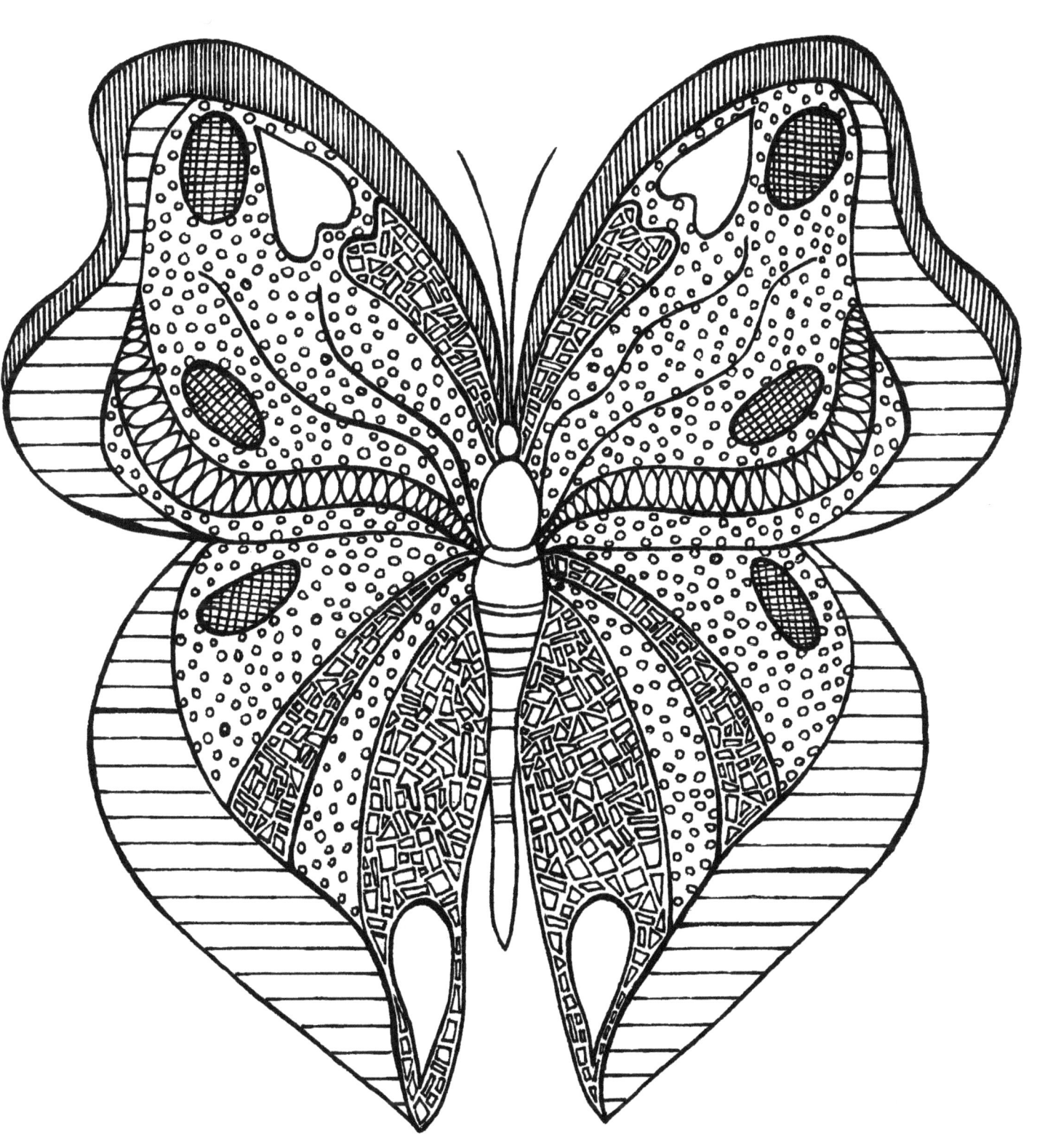

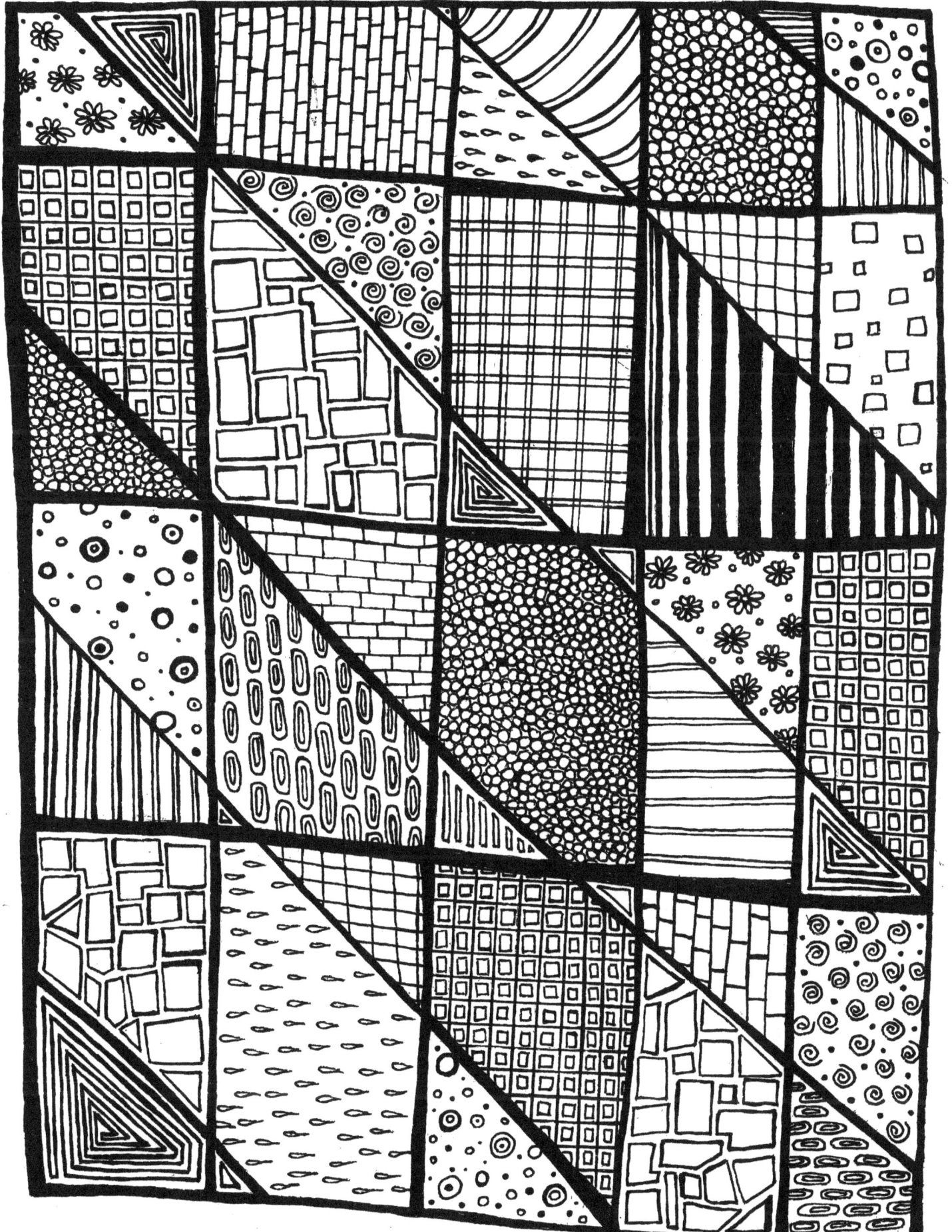

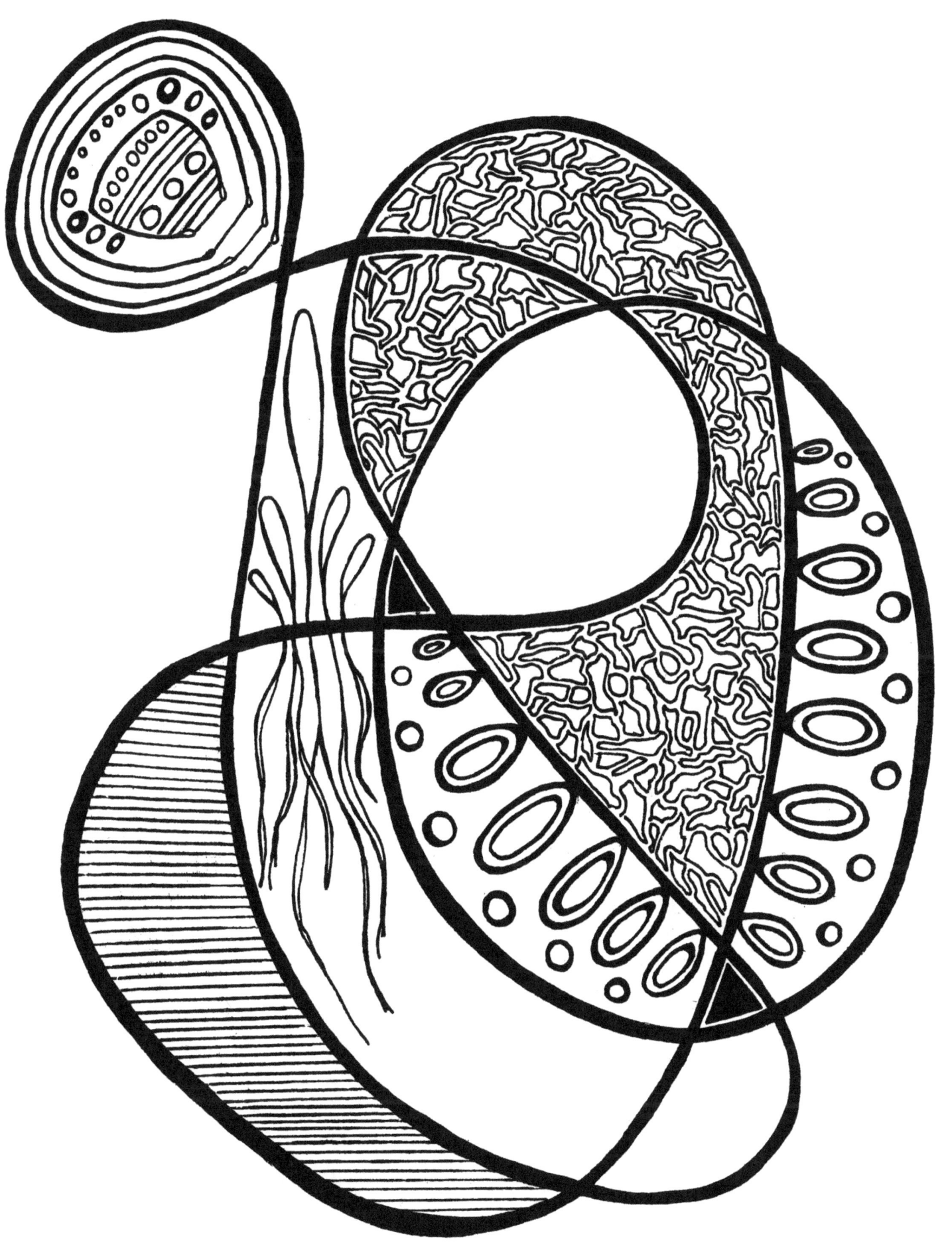

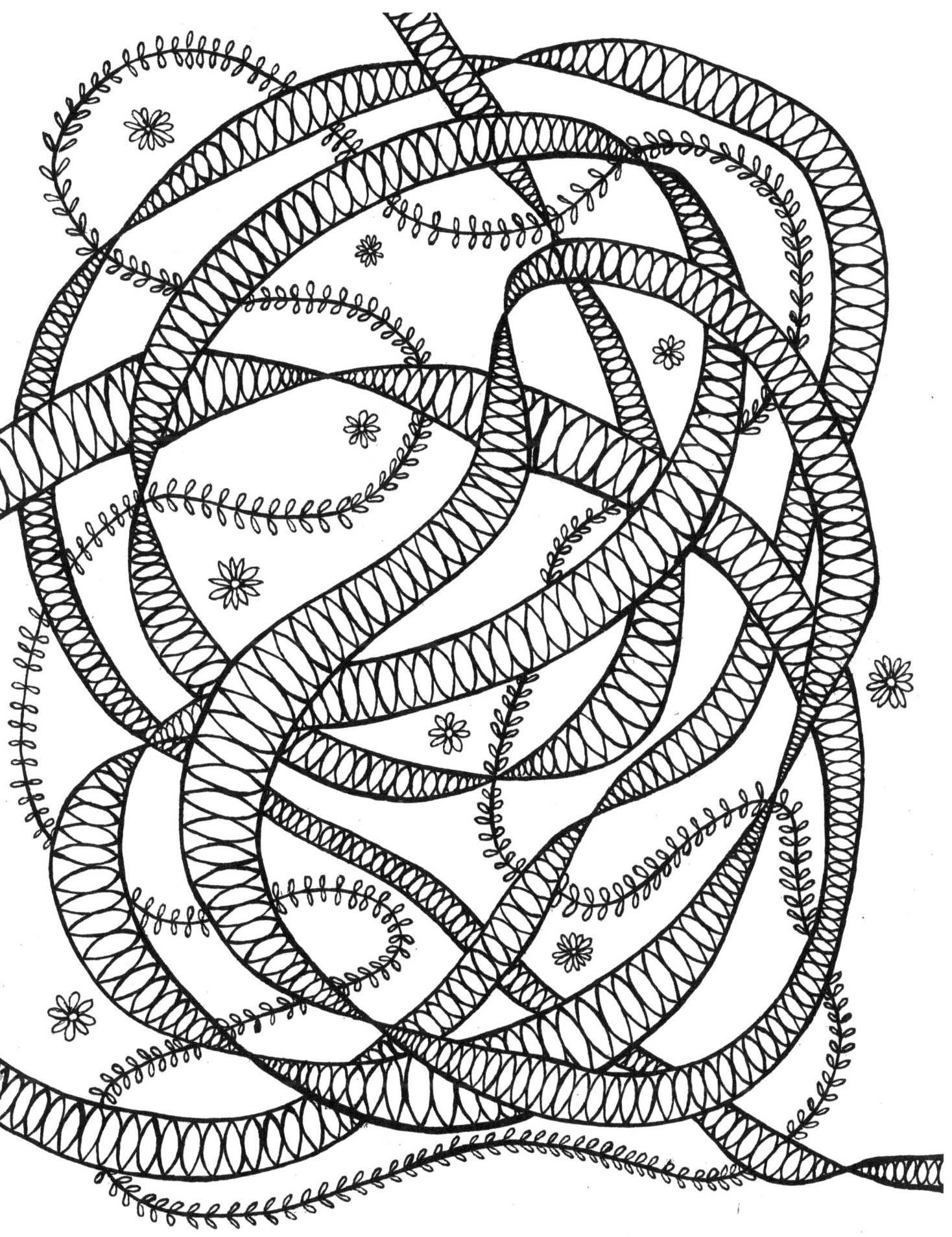

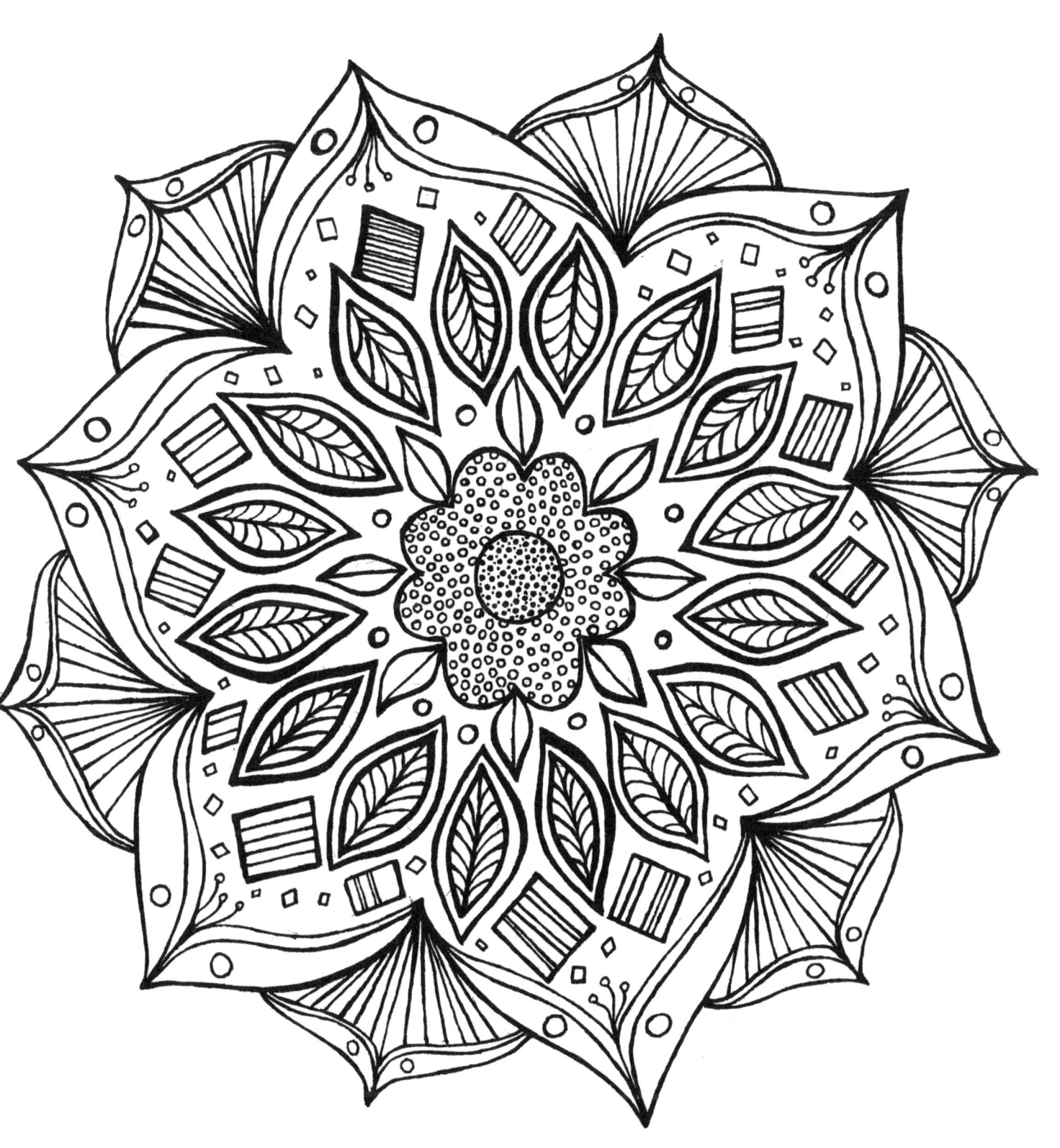

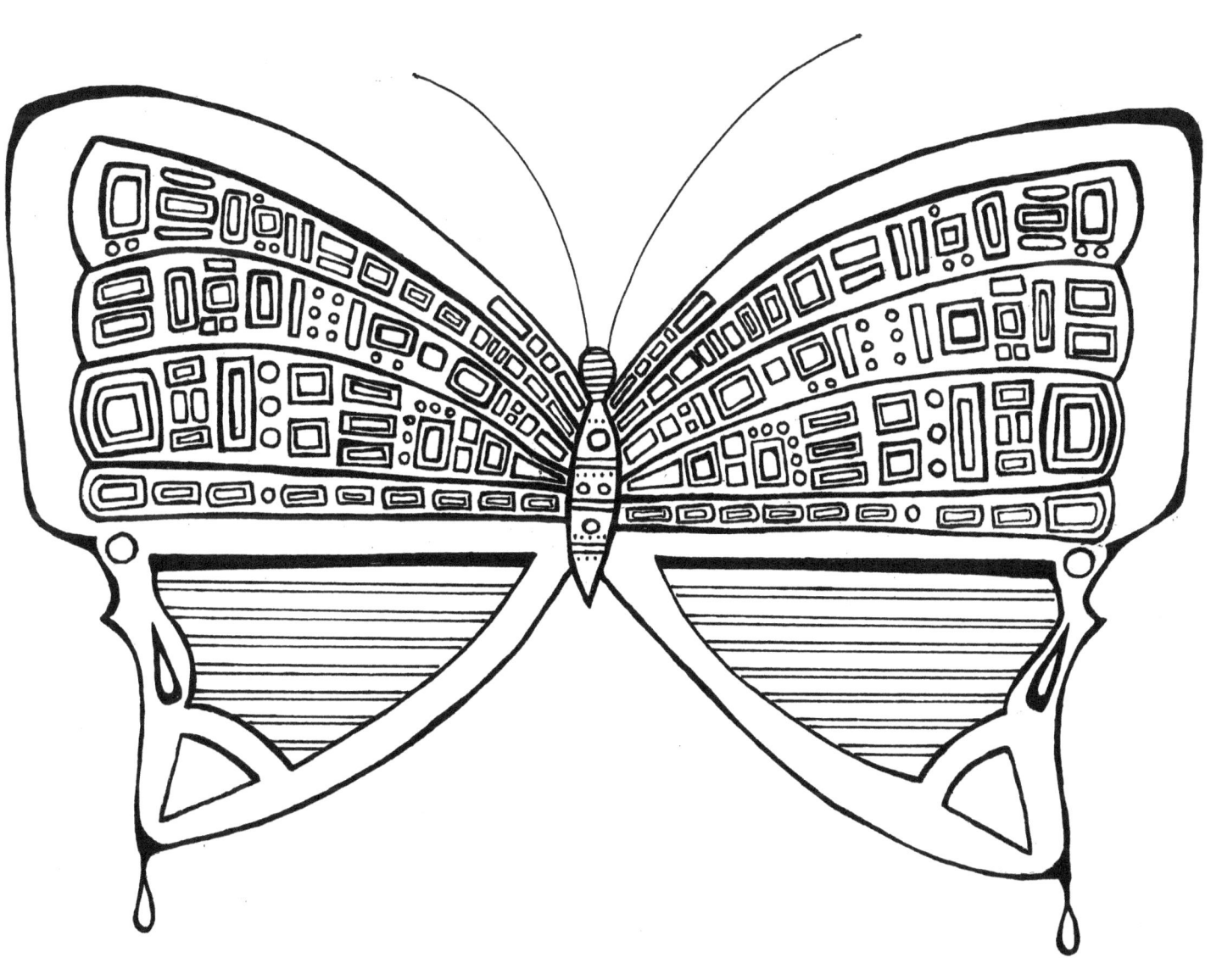

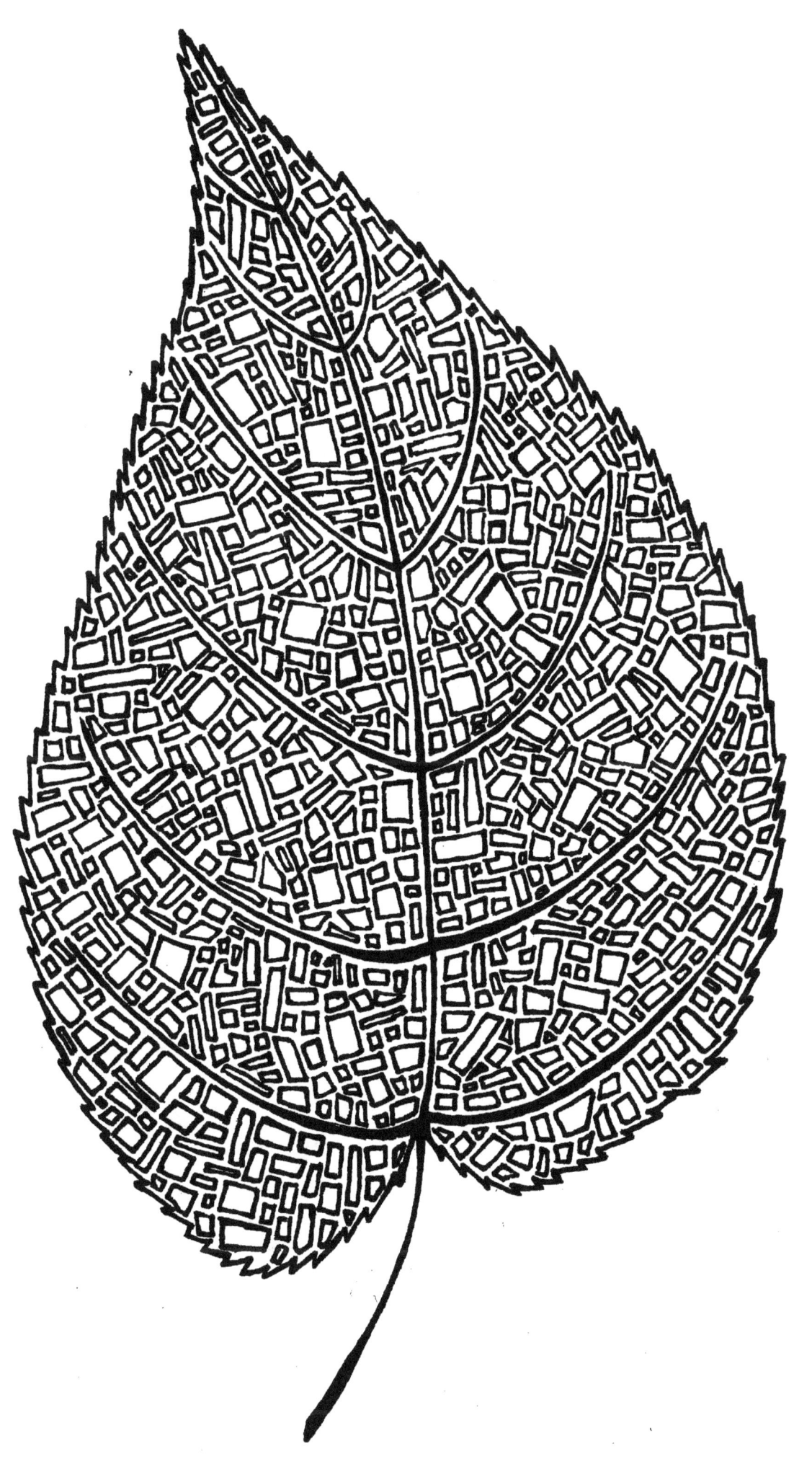

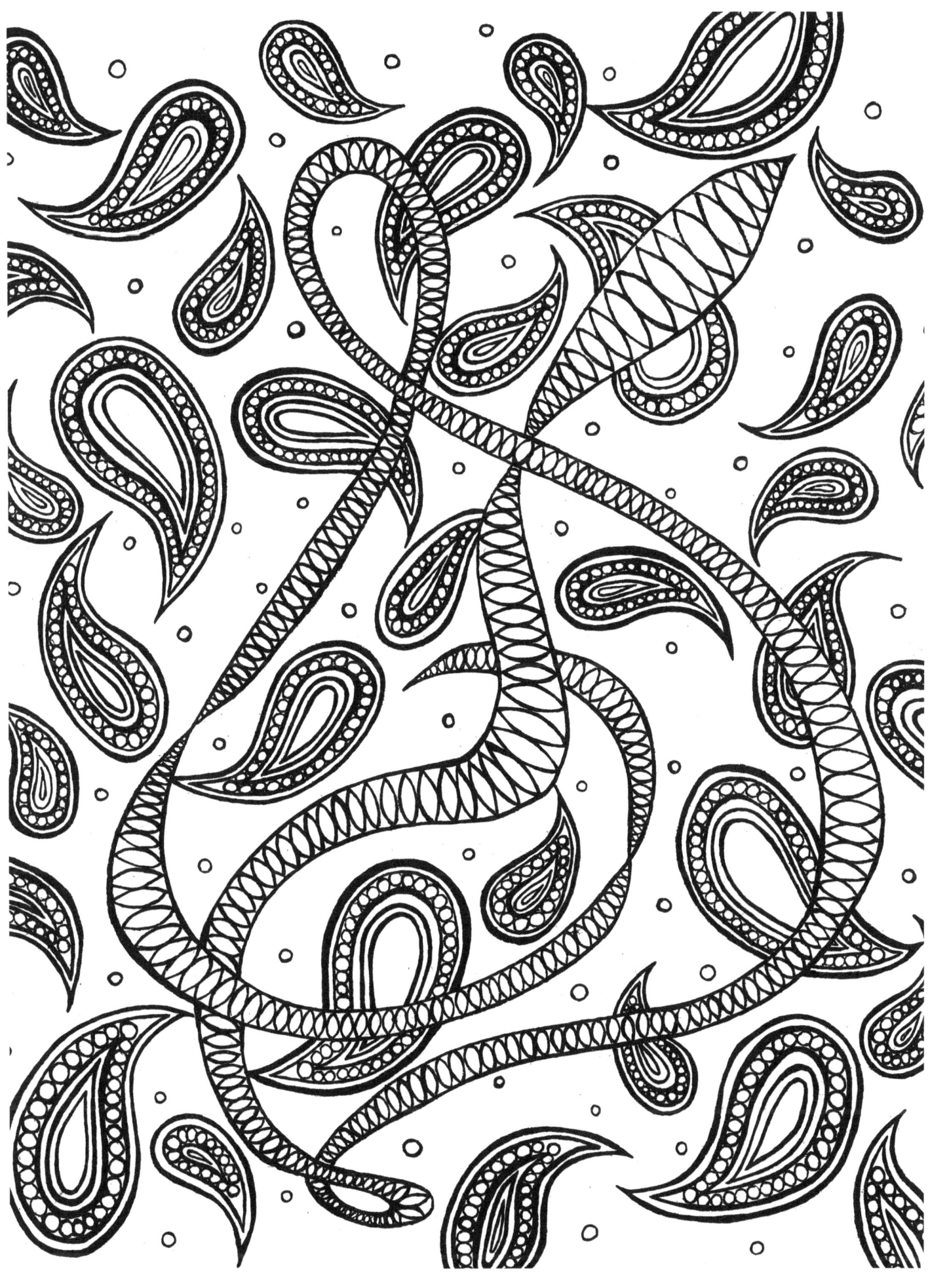

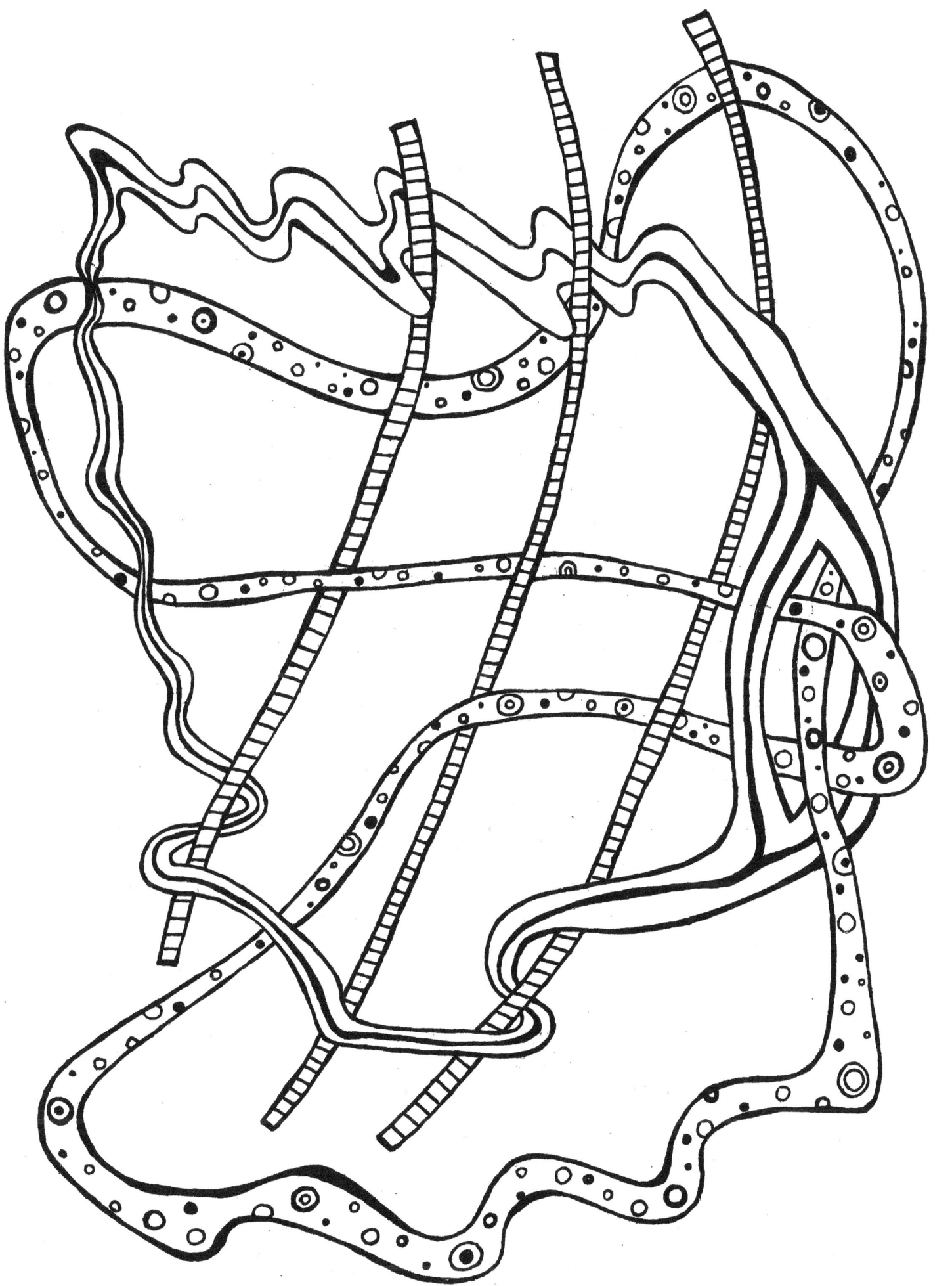

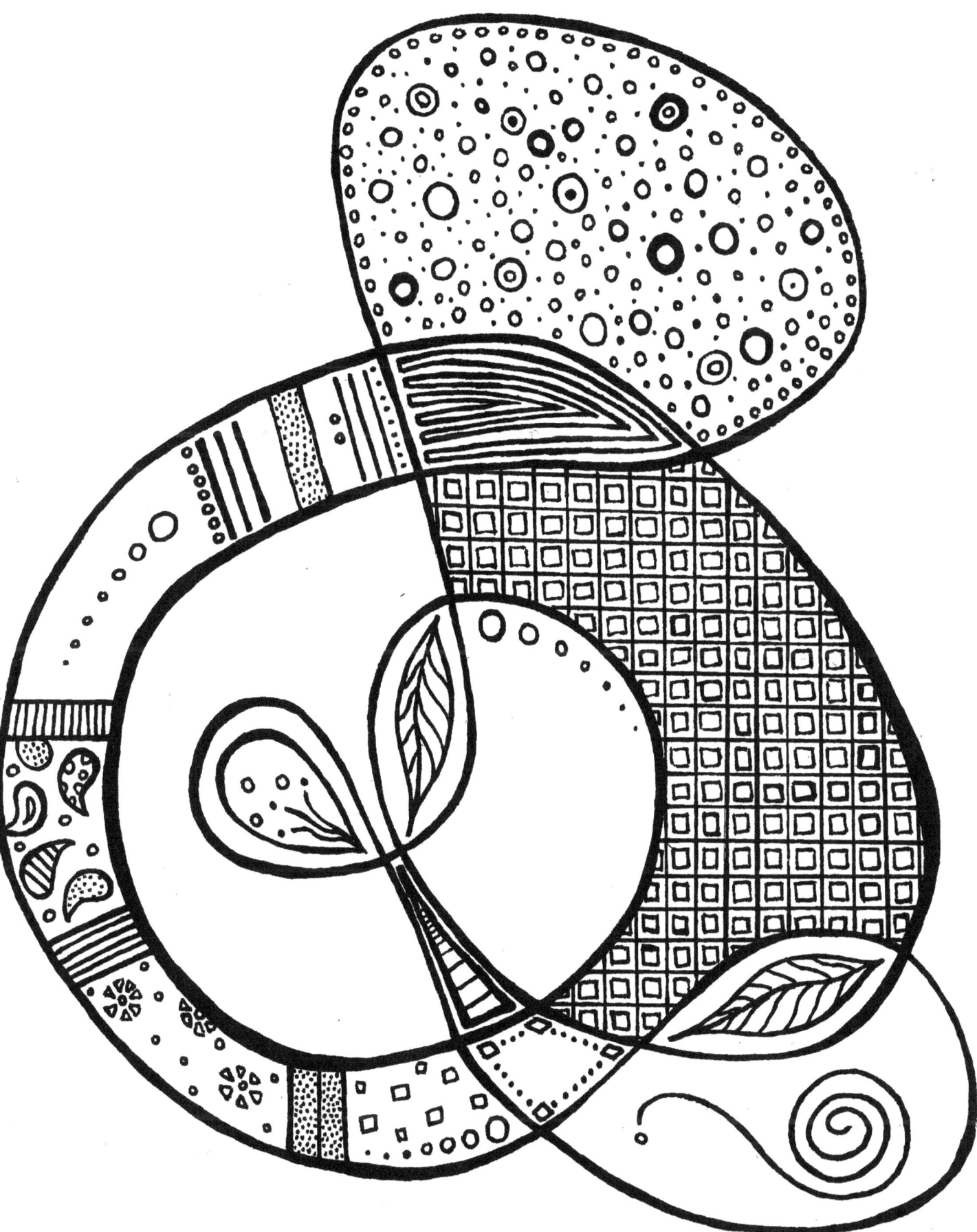

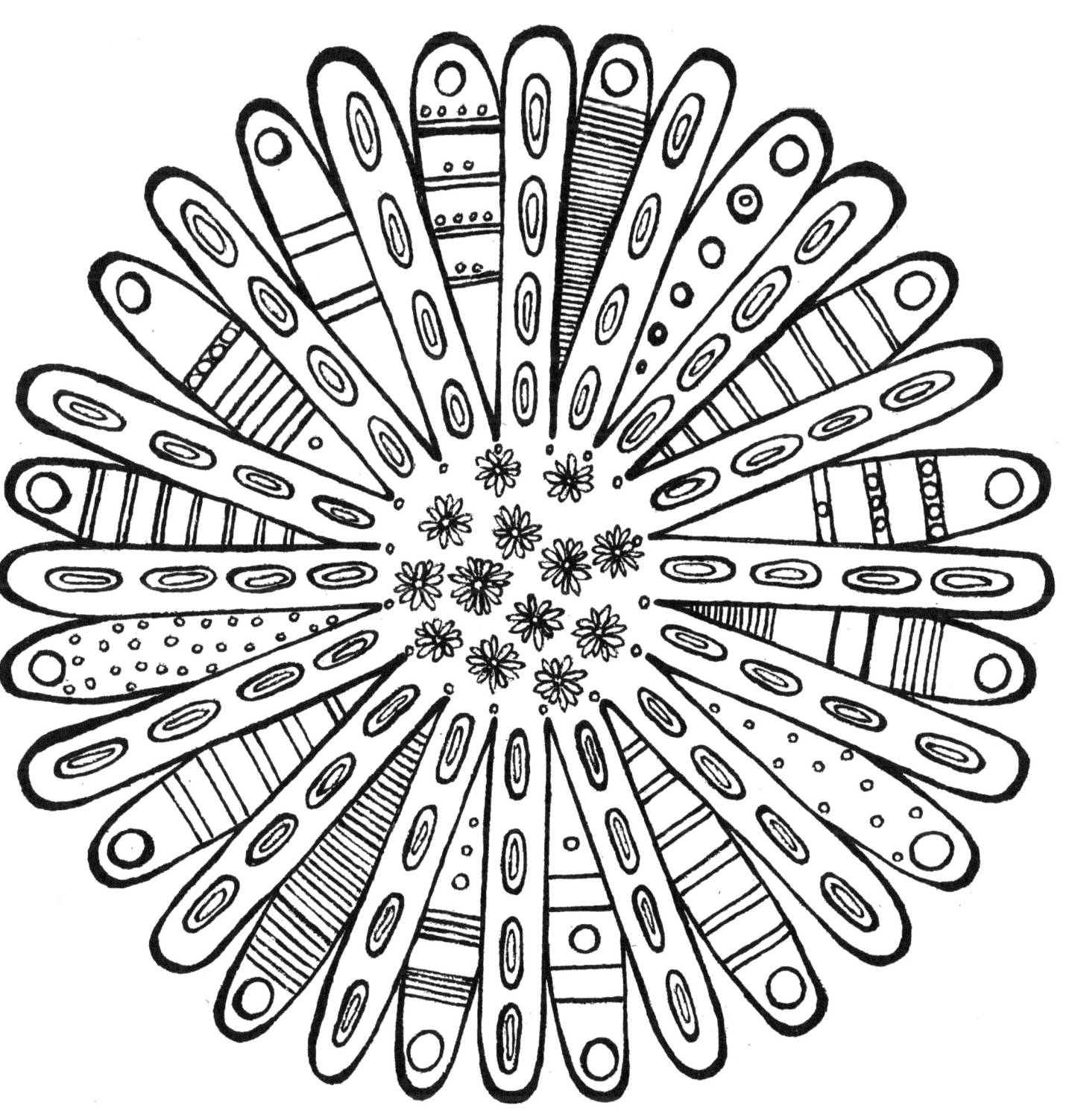

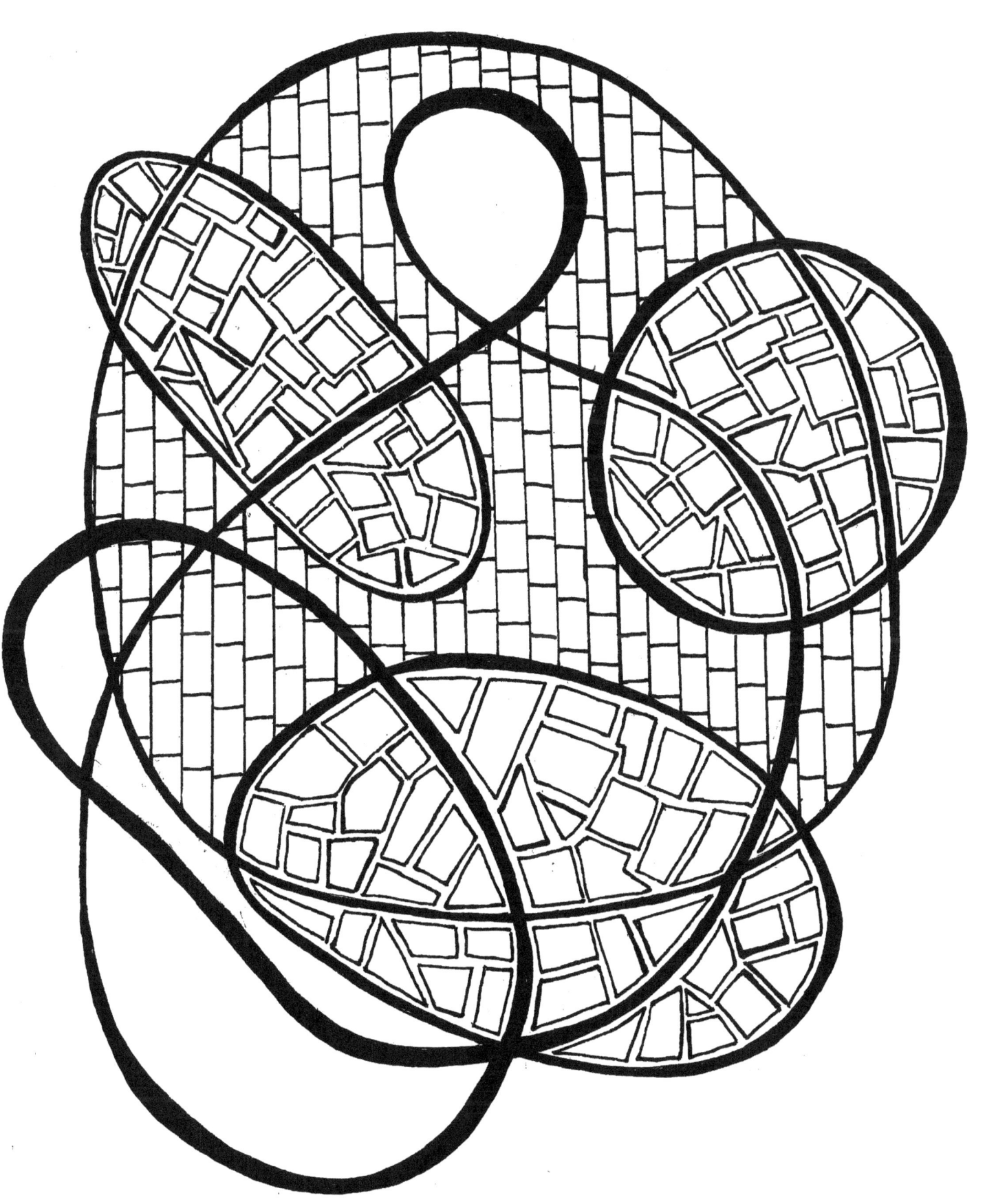

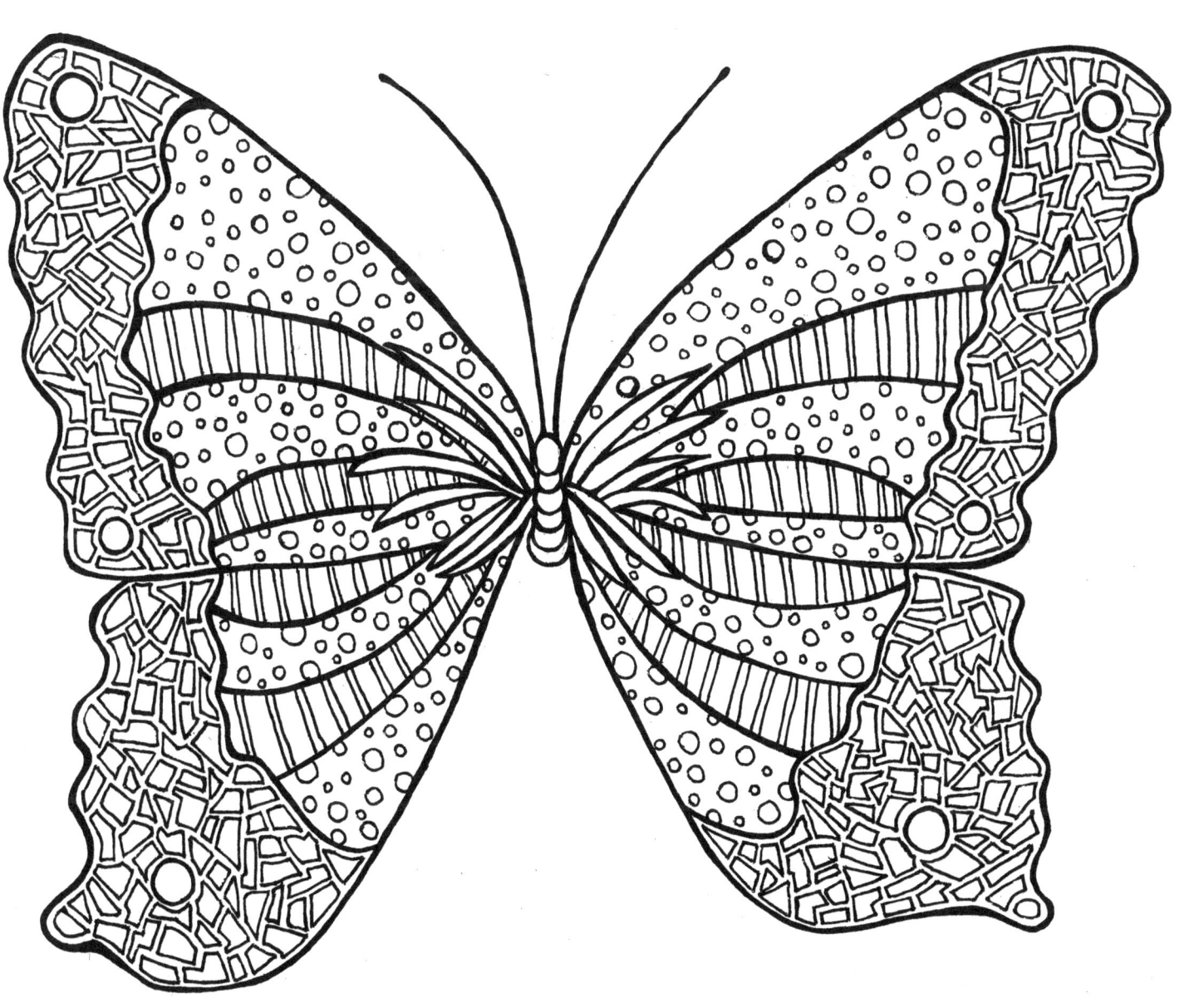

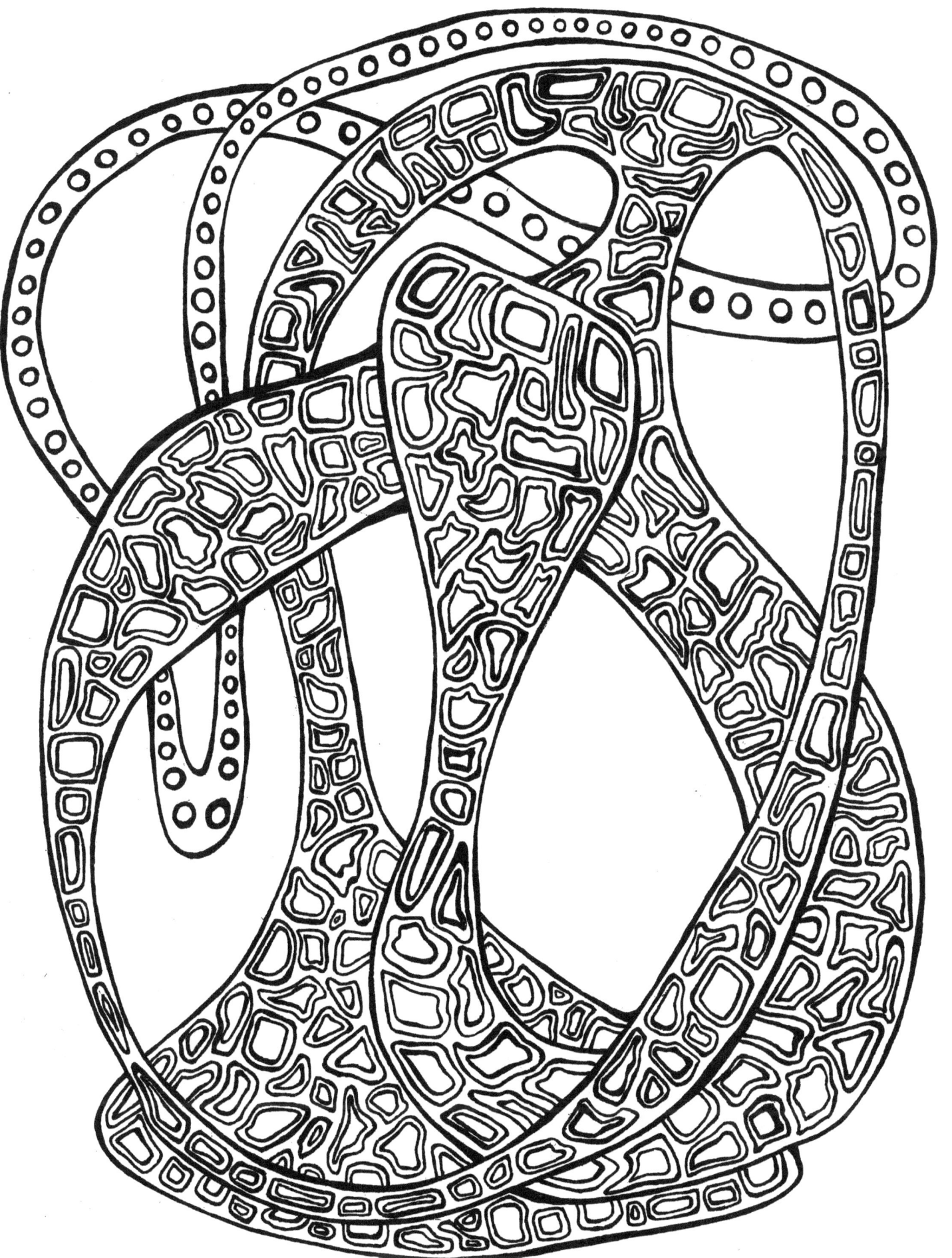

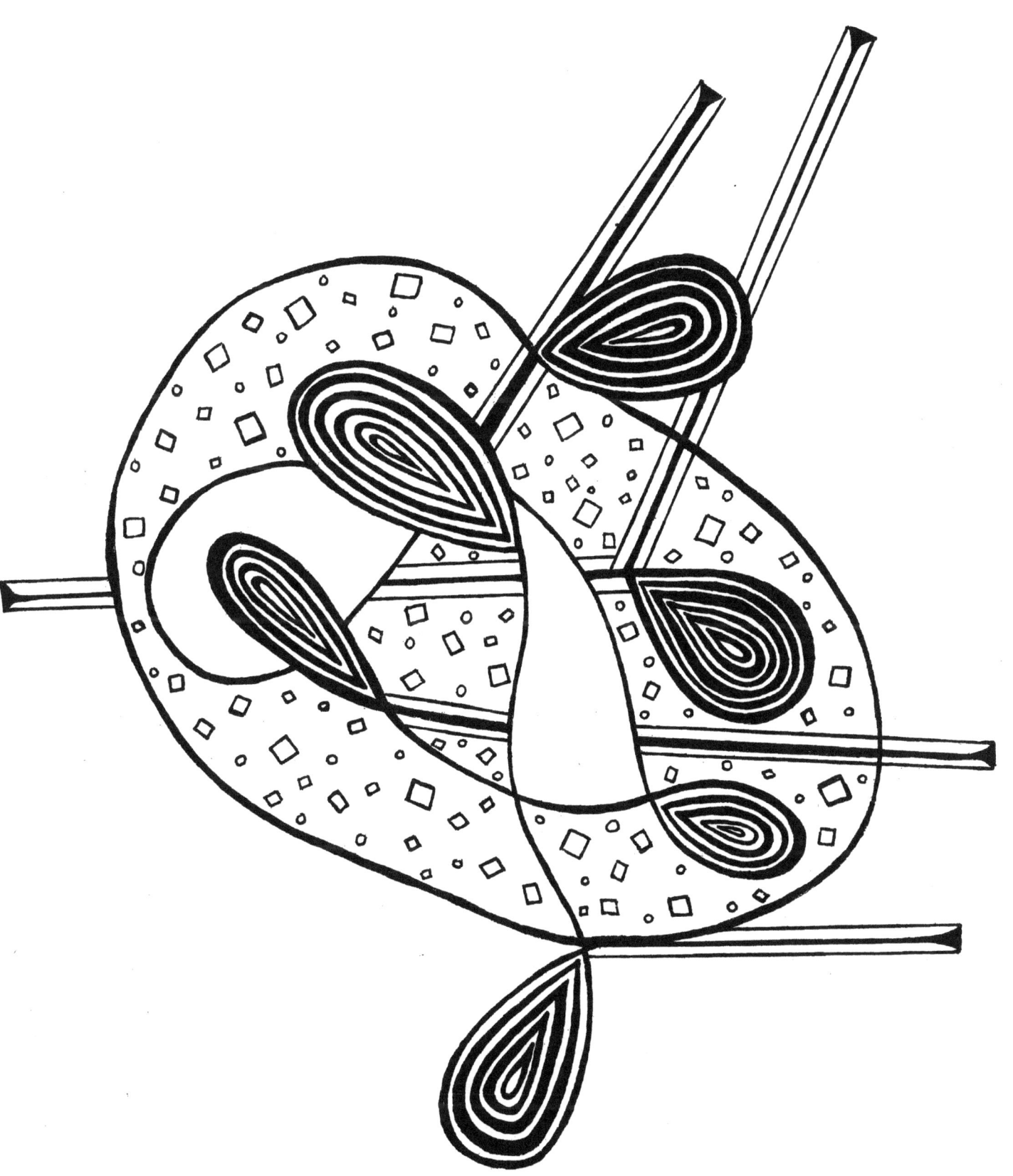

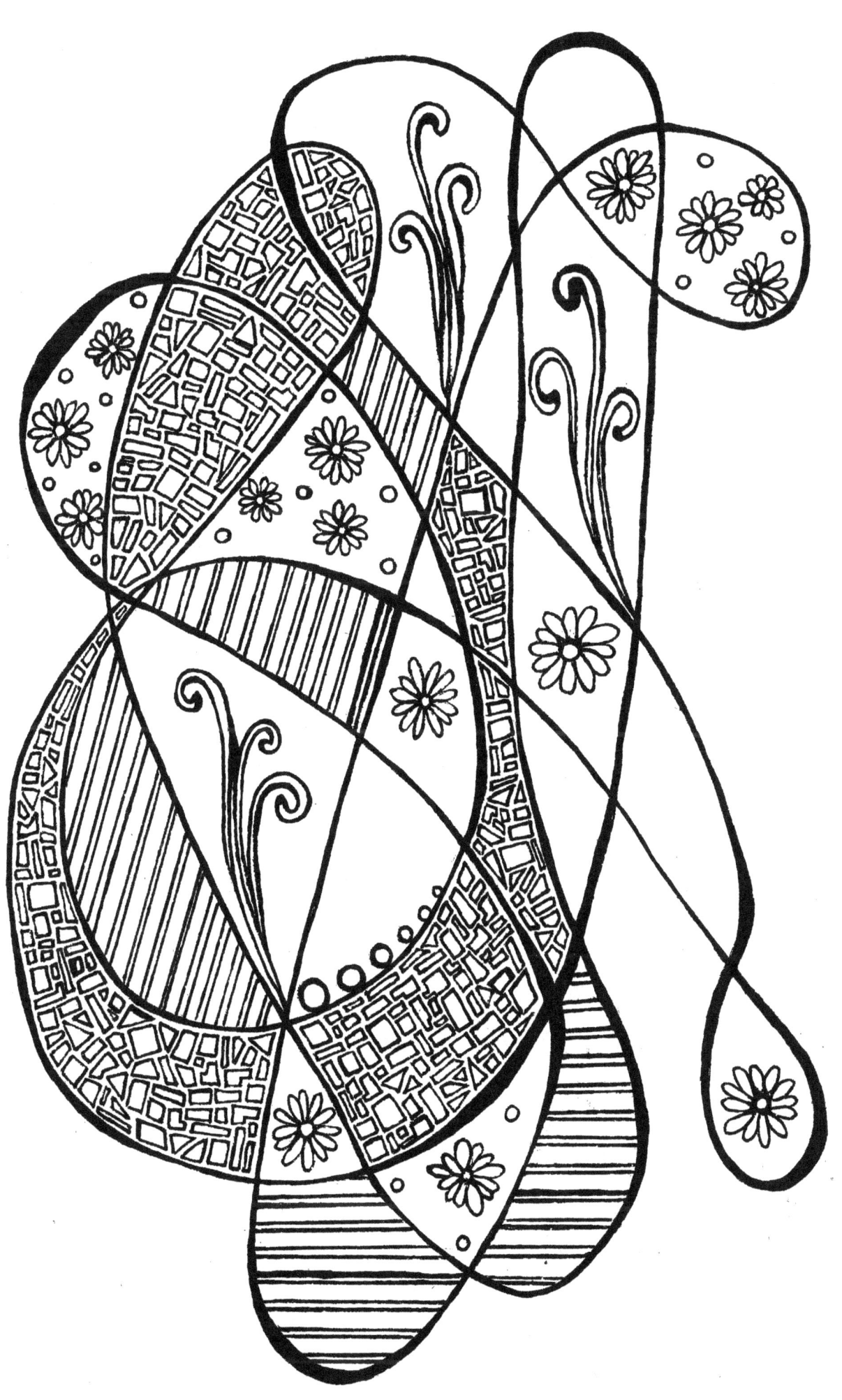

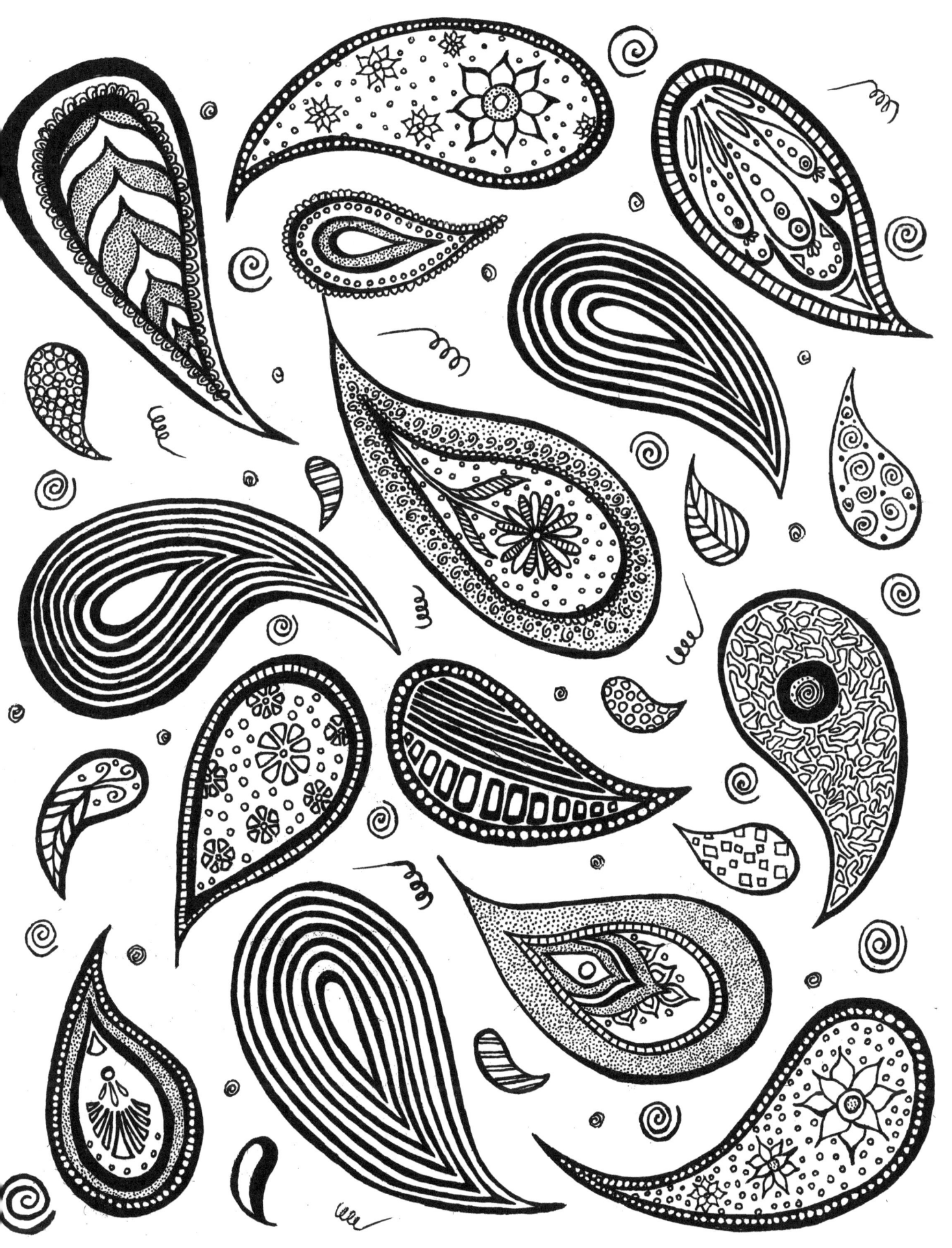

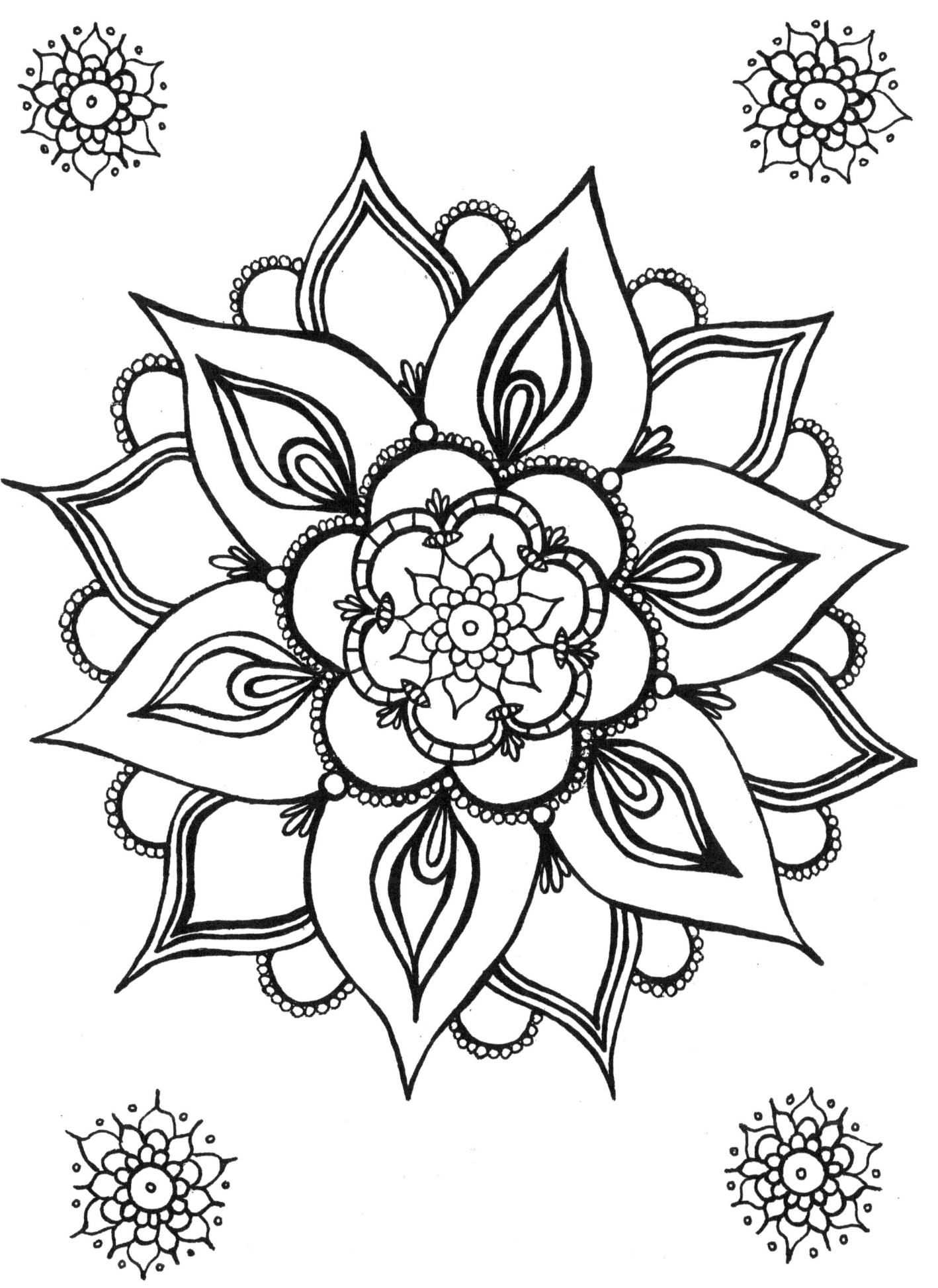

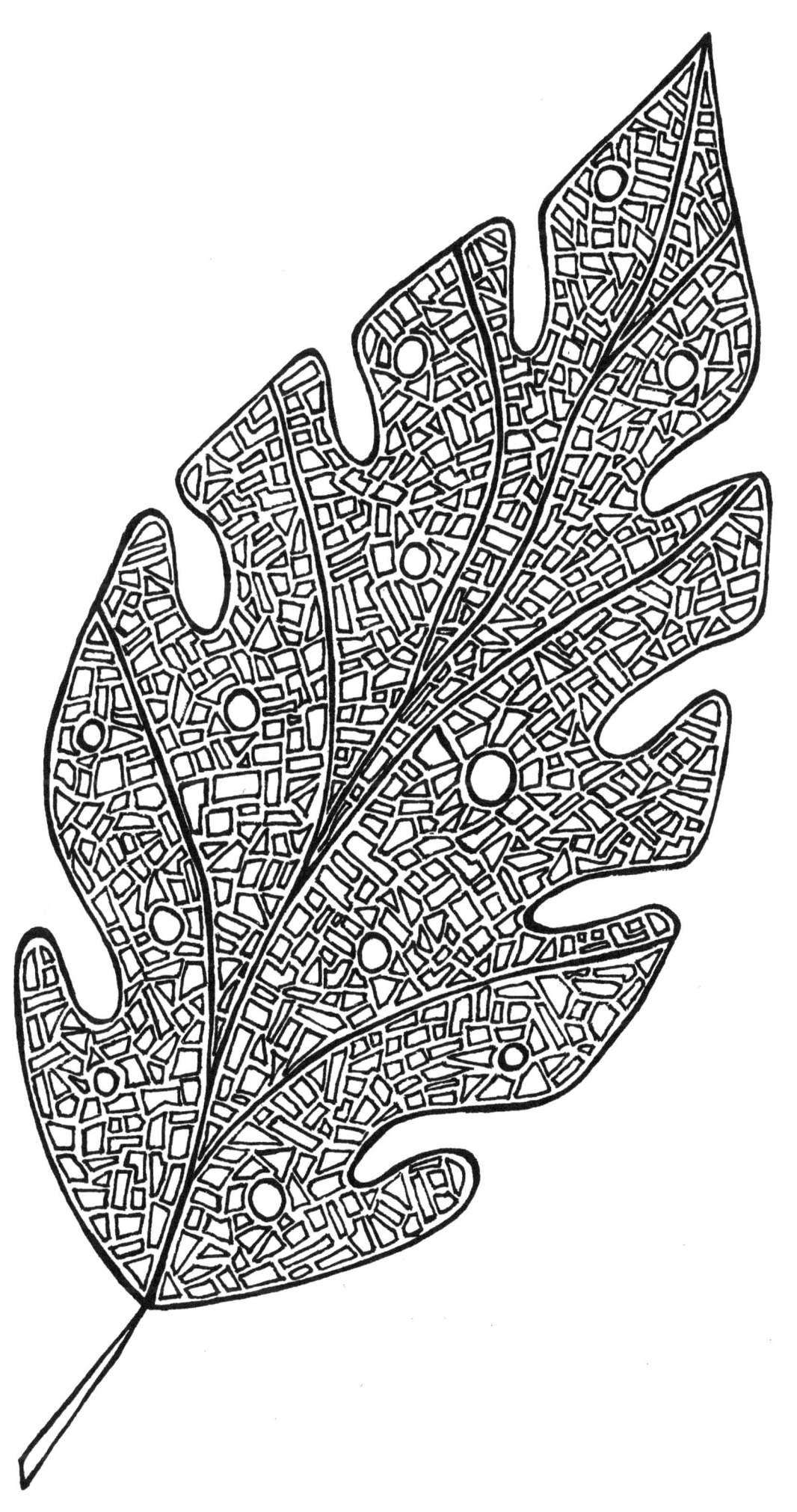

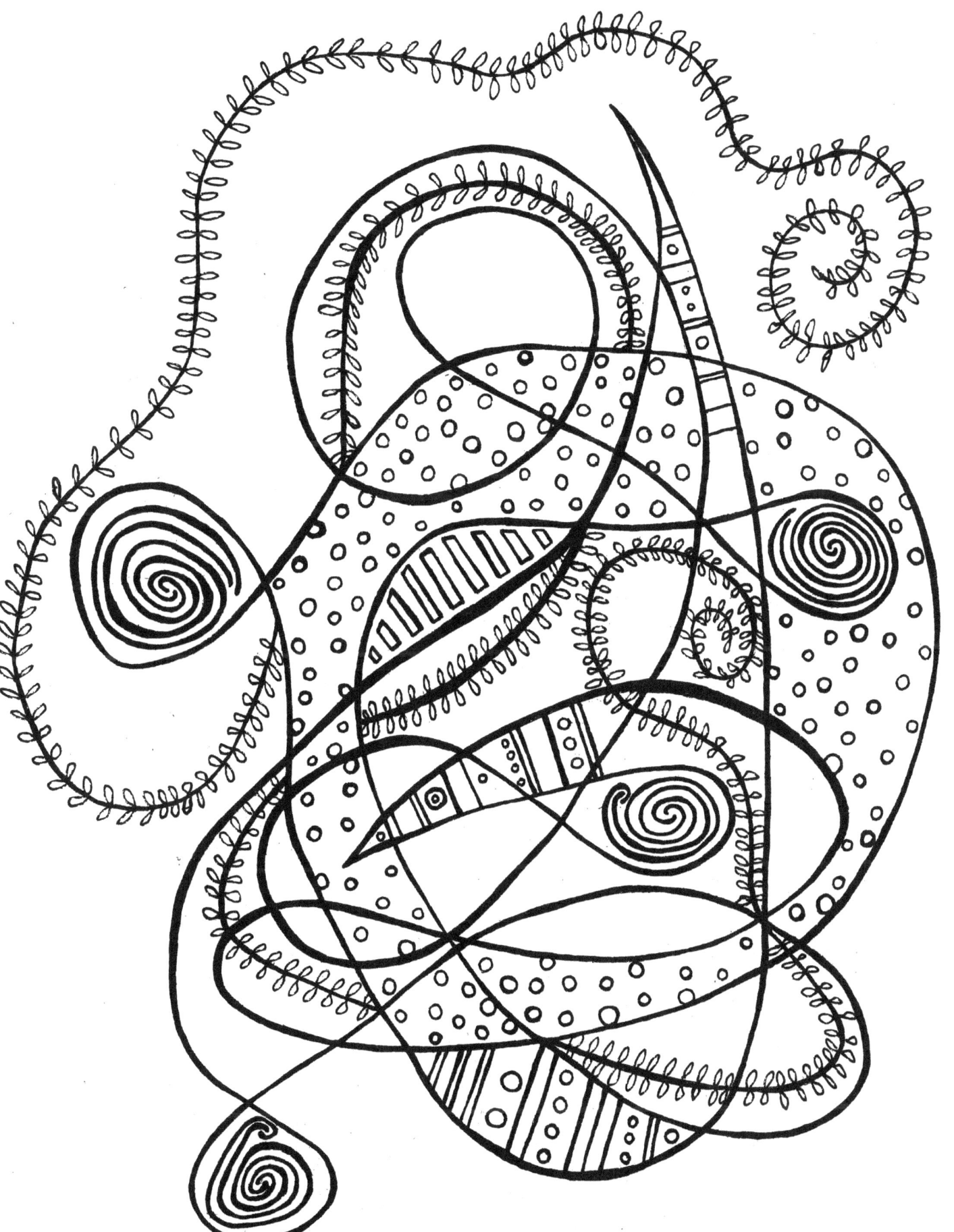

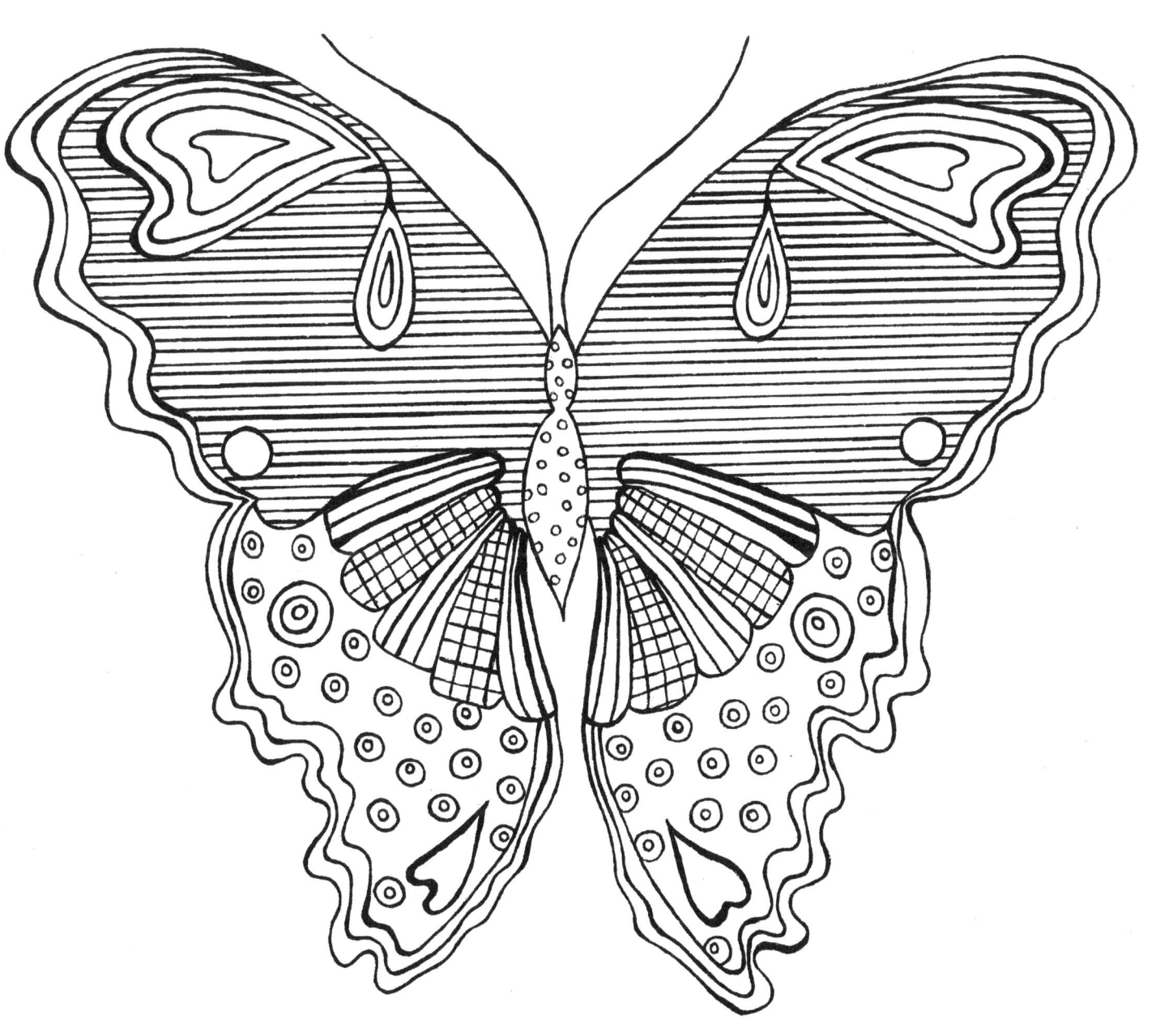

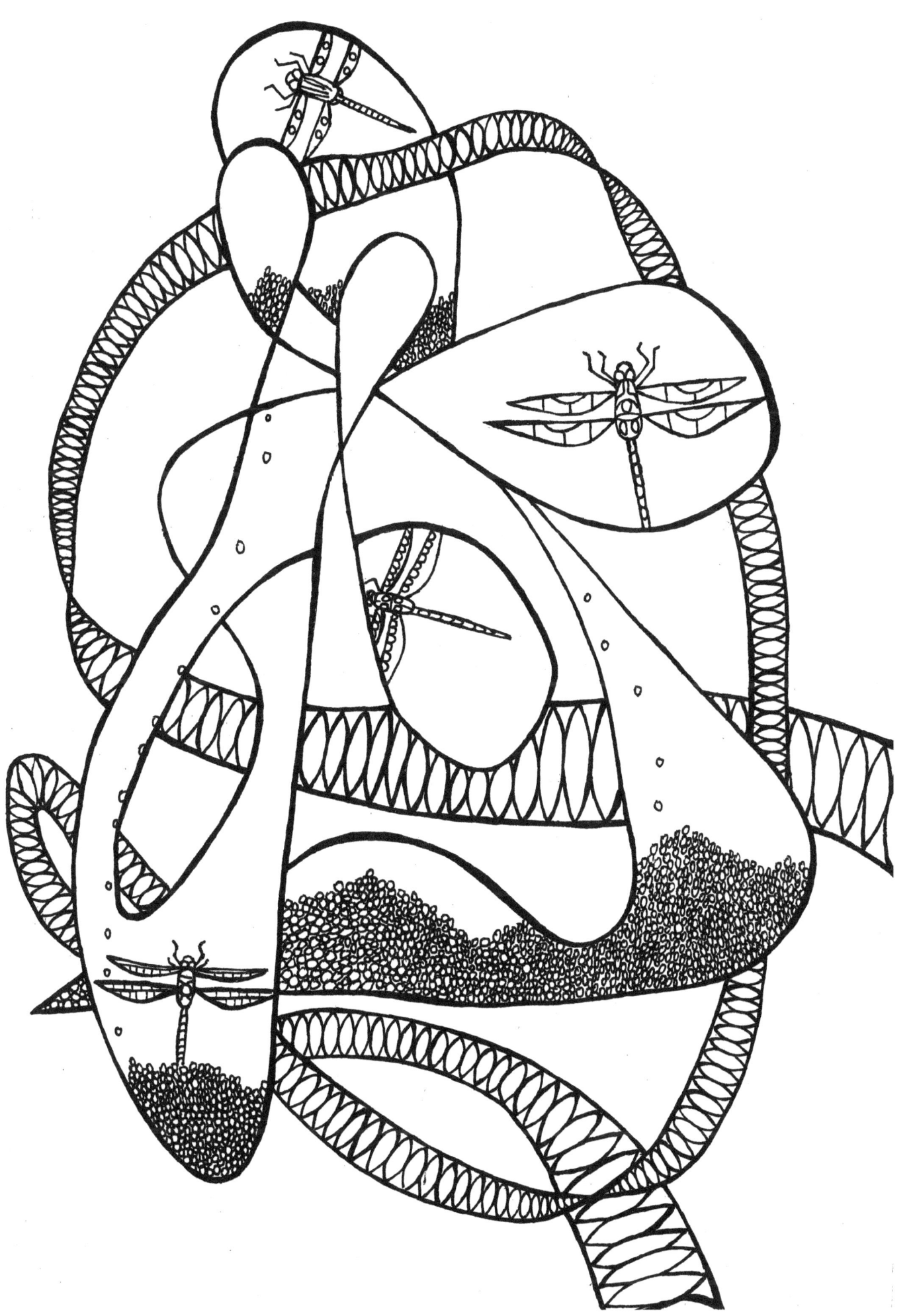

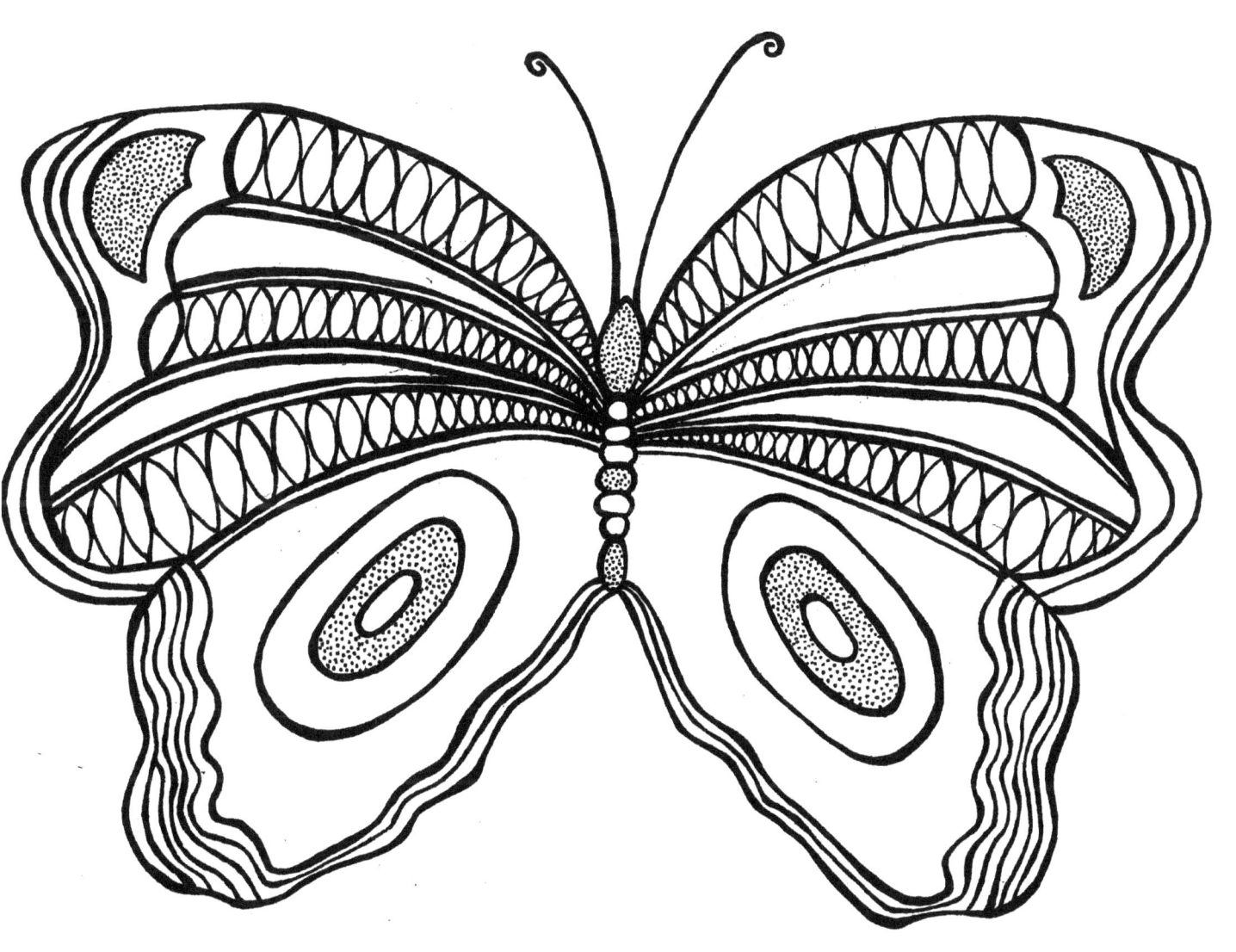

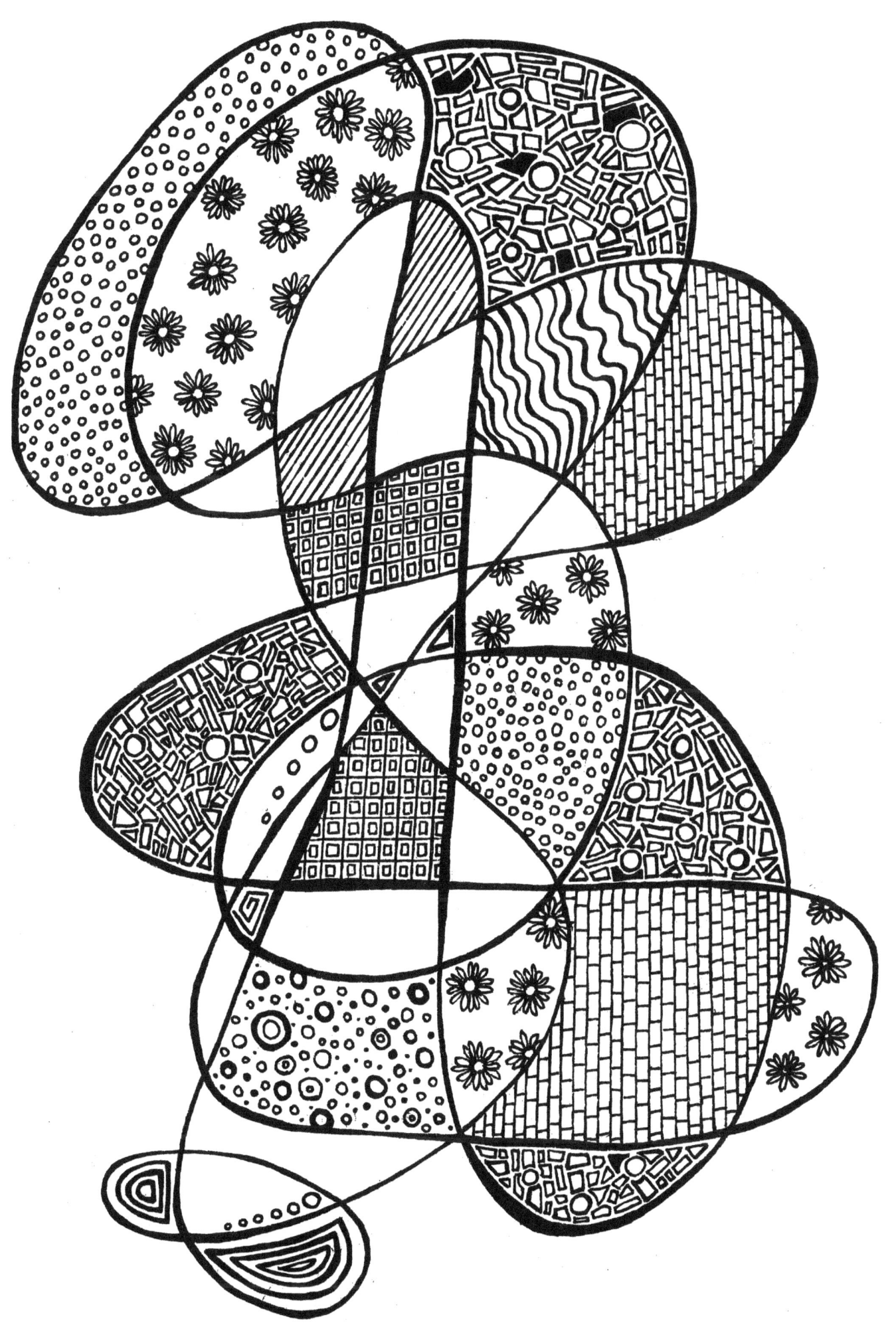

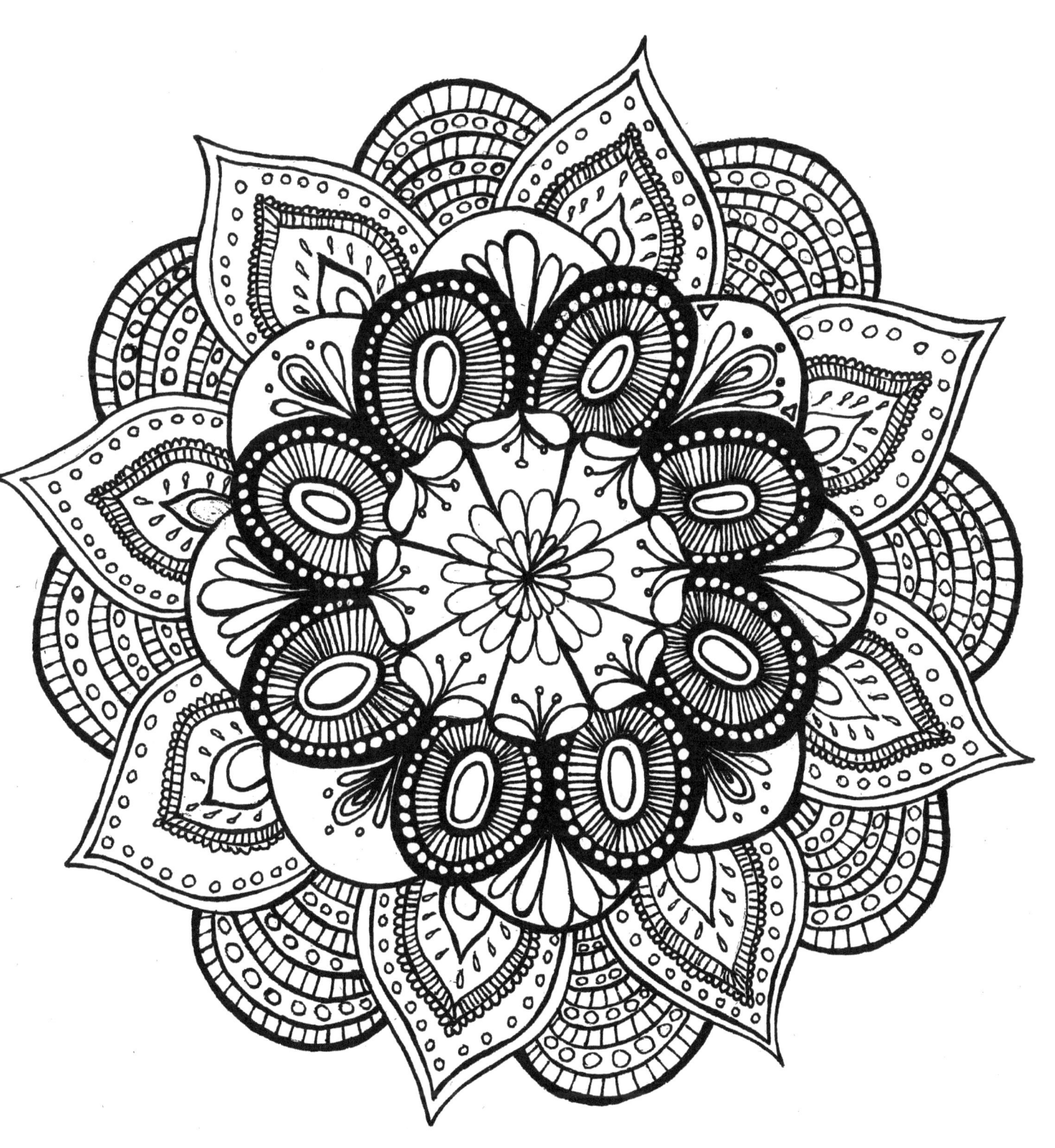

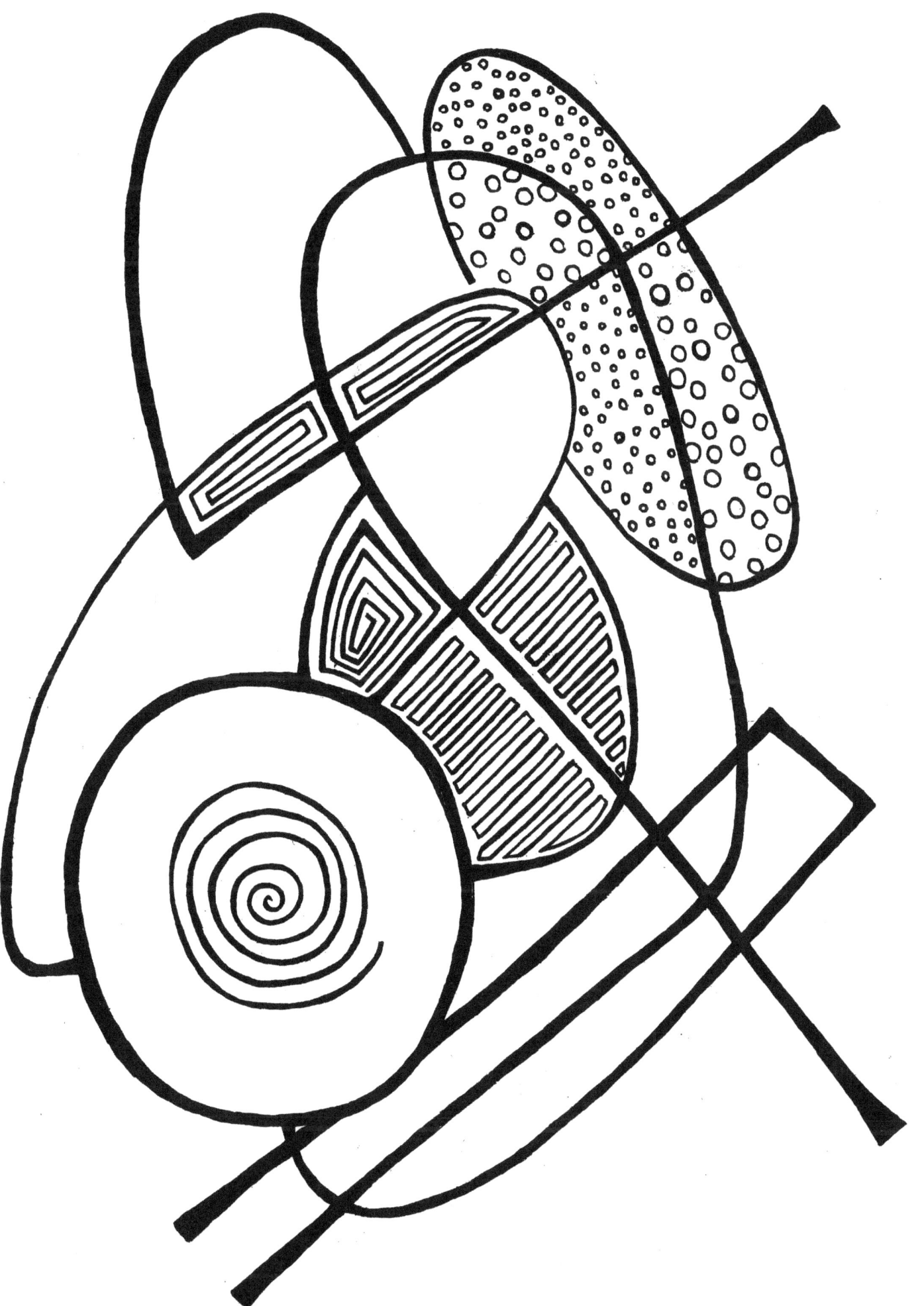